This Christmas story is dedicated to all children for their great gift of imagination, and also for the love and joy their young hearts bring to our world.

Published by Lunada Press, LLC
Torrance, CA 90505
http://www.lunadapressllc.com
Manufactured and printed in the United States of America.

Text Copyright © 2022 Jeanne Maree Iacono
Illustration Copyright © 2022 Tim Hurley

All rights reserved. No portion of this publication may be reproduced, stored in a retrieval system, or transmitted in any form or by any means electronic, mechanical, photocopying, recording or otherwise without prior written permission from the publisher.

ISBN-13: 978-0-937176-04-7

A Reading Story
& Coloring and Activity Book

Written by **Jeanne Maree Iacono**
Illustrations by **Tim Hurley**

 Look at what I see!
Birds are decorating a tree.

Let's get ready for Christmas, too.
Oh, what can we do?

Birds are Christmas helpers that fly across the sky
with golden ribbons and twinkling lights,
red ornaments, too, making trees a holiday sight.

There's holiday spirit for all who come to the zoo
and especially for YOU!

 Here's a silly, but great idea for me and you.
It will get us ready for Christmas, too.

 Rub-a-dub-dub
we're two zebras in a tub.

Silly me and silly you...
just getting ready for Christmas at the zoo!

Birds sing with glee! One zebra. Two zebras.
Zebras getting ready for Christmas, too.

Wow! You are all dressed up in green and red
from your zebra toe to your zebra head!

The giraffe looks over the fence with much surprise,
"Zebras should win the Christmas decorating prize."

Still the giraffe stands straight, proud, and tall
to show a holiday wreath around his neck to all!

At the day's end all the animals settled in for the night. Twinkling stars cast a magic upon the zoo with their light.

That night as all the animals slept
zebras dreamed
and…as only possible in dreams…
Santa was calling for his reindeer,
"Come Dancer." "Come Prancer…"

Soon two red and green-stripped zebras leapt
and were flying through the night
with a sleigh full of toys and oh yes… take a guess!
It's jolly old St. Nick, himself, seen by starlight.
Away, away zebras flew through the night.

On Christmas morning two zebras woke to surprise
as all the animals rose with wonder in their eyes.
Behold under their holiday star-topped tree
are beautifully wrapped gifts for everyone to see.

 Look there are presents for EVERYONE!

Let's have holiday zoo fun all day long!

 Happy zebras sing out: Merry Christmas to all
let's have fun until nightfall!

Some Fun Activities!

Now Let's Play!

Count the animals as you go through the maze.

1. Draw the zebras in the bathtub.
2. Color the picture.

Write your own zoo story in the open space.

The birds in the story used decorations to get the trees ready for the holiday. How many words can you make using the letters in the word below?

DECORATIONS

PARENT'S BOX: This sequencing activity will help prepare your child for reading. After your child has ordered the pictures, have them write a sentence for each picture that tells what happened in the story.

WRITE 1, 2, 3 & 4
TO SHOW WHAT HAPPENS NEXT!

Color the zebras for Christmas.

www.ingramcontent.com/pod-product-compliance
Lightning Source LLC
Chambersburg PA
CBHW061817290426
44110CB00026B/2898